How can I be a tiger?

Contents

Written by Mary Roulston

Illustrated by Szilvia Szakall

Collins

What's in this book?

Listen and say

bee

cat

monster

This is a school party. There are lots of games to play and lots of things to buy. Everyone is having fun.

I love tigers. Can I be a tiger?

5

What do you need?

Wow! Look at the children's faces! There's a butterfly, a tiger, a cat, a monster and a bee!

How do you do face painting? Let's see ...

You need these.

brush

sponge

face paints

water

Let's paint a tiger

You need orange, white and black face paints.

Use a sponge. Put some water on the sponge. Paint the top part of the face orange. Paint the bottom part of the face white.

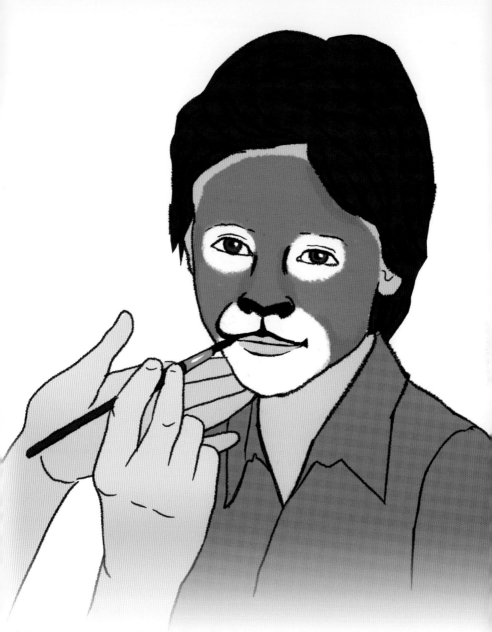

Now, use a brush. Paint the tiger's eyes white. Paint the nose and the mouth black.

line

Paint black lines on the face.

Look! Now you're a beautiful tiger!
Can you make a tiger noise?

Let's paint a butterfly

You need black and any colours you like.

Paint a black butterfly body on the nose.
Its body is long and thin.

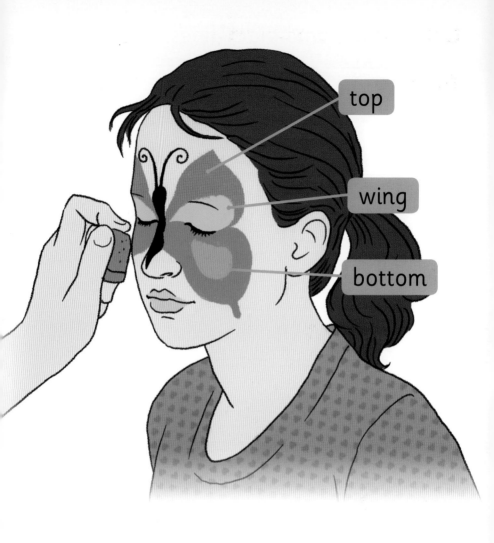

top

wing

bottom

Draw four butterfly wings on the face.
The bottom wings are bigger than
the top wings. Now, paint the wings some
beautiful colours!

Finish with some black lines.

What colours would you like for your butterfly? Do you want pink or blue? You can choose any colours!

Look! You're a pretty butterfly.
Can you fly?

15

Let's paint a monster

You need green, black and white face paints.

Paint all the face green. Now, paint the eyes and mouth black.

This monster has got big white teeth.
Look! You're a monster! Oh, no! Let's run!

Let's paint a cat

You need white, black, pink and grey face paints.

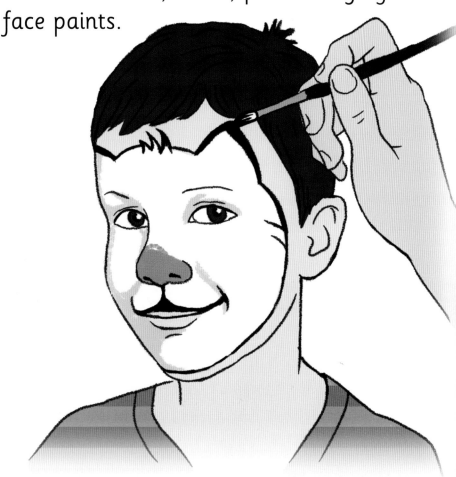

Paint all the face white. Use a brush.
Draw two ear shapes.

Paint the nose pink.

Draw black lines on the mouth.
Colour the ear shapes pink or grey.

What a nice cat! *Meow!*

Let's paint a bee

You need yellow, black and white
face paints.

Paint a yellow and black bee body on
the nose. Paint a yellow bee head.

Now, paint two white wings.

Look at all the beautiful faces!
You can be a tiger, too!

Which do you like the best?

Picture dictionary

Listen and repeat

body

ear

eye

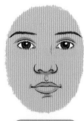

face

head

mouth

nose

wing

1 Look and order

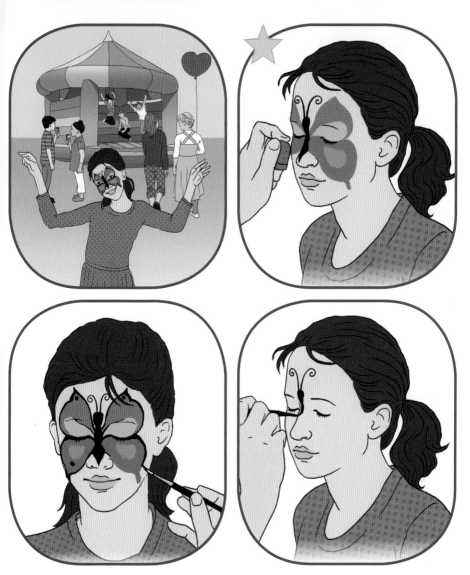

2 Listen and say

Collins

Published by Collins
An imprint of HarperCollins*Publishers*
Westerhill Road
Bishopbriggs
Glasgow
G64 2QT

HarperCollins*Publishers*
1st Floor, Watermarque Building
Ringsend Road
Dublin 4
Ireland

William Collins' dream of knowledge for all began with the publication of his first book in 1819.

A self-educated mill worker, he not only enriched millions of lives, but also founded a flourishing publishing house. Today, staying true to this spirit, Collins books are packed with inspiration, innovation and practical expertise. They place you at the centre of a world of possibility and give you exactly what you need to explore it.

10 9 8 7 6 5 4 3 2

ISBN 978-0-00-839841-5

Collins® and COBUILD® are registered trademarks of HarperCollins*Publishers* Limited

www.collins.co.uk/elt

British Library Cataloguing in Publication Data

A catalogue record for this publication is available from the British Library.

Author: Mary Roulston
Illustrator: Szilvia Szakall (Beehive)
Series editor: Rebecca Adlard
Publishing manager: Lisa Todd
Product managers: Caroline Green and Jennifer Hall
In-house editor: Alma Puts Keren
Project manager: Emily Hooton
Editor: Barbara MacKay
Proofreaders: Natalie Murray and Michael Lamb
Cover designer: Kevin Robbins
Typesetter: 2Hoots Publishing Services Ltd
Audio produced by id audio, London
Reading guide author: Emma Wilkinson
Production controller: Rachel Weaver
Printed and bound by: GPS Group, Slovenia

MIX
Paper from
responsible sources
FSC™ C007454

This book is produced from independently certified FSC™ paper to ensure responsible forest management.

For more information visit: **www.harpercollins.co.uk/green**

Download the audio for this book and a reading guide for parents and teachers at www.collins.co.uk/839841